MILITARY MISSIONS

PEACEKEEPING

BY NEL YOMTOV

EPIC

BELLWETHER MEDIA • MINNEAPOLIS, MN

EPIC BOOKS are no ordinary books. They burst with intense action, high-speed heroics, and shadows of the unknown. Are you ready for an Epic adventure?

This edition first published in 2017 by Bellwether Media, Inc.

No part of this publication may be reproduced in whole or in part without written permission of the publisher.
For information regarding permission, write to Bellwether Media, Inc., Attention: Permissions Department, 5357 Penn Avenue South, Minneapolis, MN 55419.

Library of Congress Cataloging-in-Publication Data

Names: Yomtov, Nelson, author.
Title: Peacekeeping / by Nel Yomtov.
Description: Minneapolis, MN : Bellwether Media, Inc., 2017. | Series: Epic:
    Military Missions | Includes bibliographical references and index.
Identifiers: LCCN 2016002002 | ISBN 9781626174368 (hardcover
: alk. paper)
Subjects: LCSH: Peacekeeping forces–Juvenile literature.
Classification: LCC JZ6374 .Y66 2017 | DDC 355.4–dc23
LC record available at http://lccn.loc.gov/2016002002

Printed in the United States of America, North Mankato, MN.

TABLE OF CONTENTS

On the Job	4
The Mission	8
The Plan	12
The Team	16
Accomplished!	20
Glossary	22
To Learn More	23
Index	24

ON THE JOB

A team of United States Army soldiers serves in Afghanistan. The group comes across some **land mines**. The soldiers must blow them up so no one will get hurt.

UZBEKISTAN

TAJIKISTAN

TURKMENISTAN

AFGHANISTAN

N
W ✛ E
S

IRAN

PAKISTAN

The team puts small bombs around the mines. The soldiers move far away and set off the bombs.

The mines go off, too. Now the area is safe for the local people!

THE MISSION

It is difficult for some countries to heal after a war. Their governments may be weak.

They want safety for their people. But sometimes they need help to create peace.

A WORLDWIDE TASK

Peacekeepers serve in trouble spots all around the world.

Many countries send soldiers to help. These troops are called peacekeepers.

They train police and military members. They often work with both sides of a **conflict** to stop the fighting.

REAL-LIFE PEACEKEEPING

What: Peacekeeping between Egypt and Israel

Who: Task Force Sinai

Where: Sinai Peninsula, Egypt

When: Ongoing since 1982

Why: Help uphold a peace agreement signed by Egypt and Israel in 1979 after years of fighting

How: U.S. troops guard the border between Egypt and Israel; the U.S. provides security, military training, and resources to keep people in both countries safe.

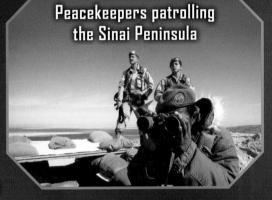

Peacekeepers patrolling the Sinai Peninsula

THE PLAN

Peacekeepers watch over people and activities. **Binoculars** and **night-vision goggles** help them keep an eye out for danger.

night-vision goggles

binoculars

MQ-9 Reaper drone

They may also use **drones** to gather information.

UNITED WE STAND

U.S. troops often work with the United Nations (U.N.). The U.N. works with many countries to build peace.

Soldiers on these missions hope not to fight. But they are armed. They carry guns and drive in **armored** vehicles. They can use force against people who cause trouble.

THE TEAM

Peacekeepers teach and train others. They share knowledge with other countries' armies.

SOLDIER PROFILE

A peacekeeping soldier must be:

- Brave
- Intelligent
- Cool under pressure
- Caring
- Willing to work with different groups
- Able to use weapons and machinery

Sometimes they stand guard to keep buildings or government leaders safe.

Many skills are needed to be a peacekeeper. Those who serve are well-trained soldiers.

They know how to work closely with local armies. Some learn new languages to talk with local people.

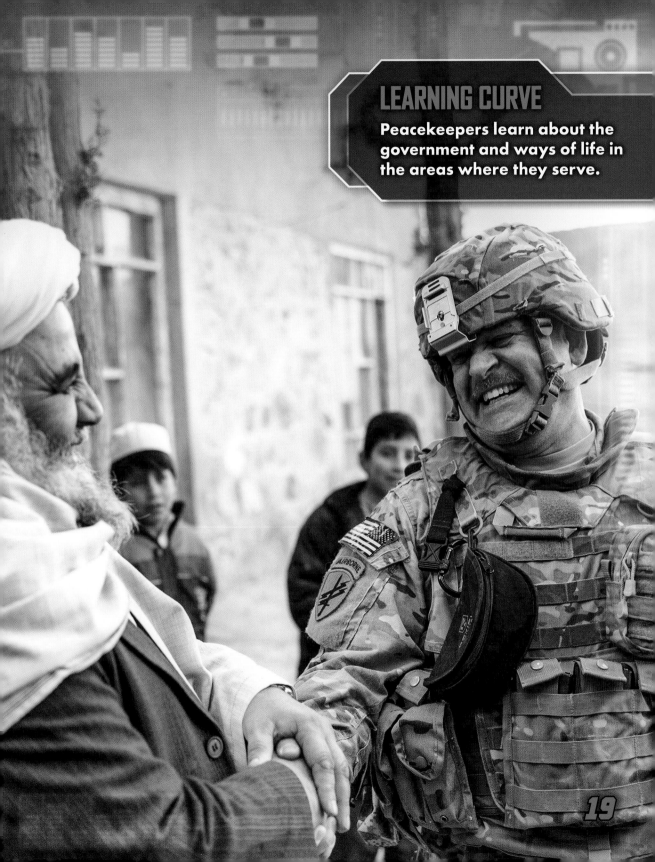

LEARNING CURVE

Peacekeepers learn about the government and ways of life in the areas where they serve.

19

ACCOMPLISHED!

After times of war, countries need time to rebuild. Peacekeepers use their skills to help as many people as they can.

Missions of peace make the world a safer place!

GLOSSARY

armored—covered in thick plates for protection

binoculars—handheld tools that let soldiers see things that are far away

conflict—a war or period of fighting

drones—unmanned military aircraft controlled by remotes

land mines—bombs buried in the ground that explode when stepped on or driven over

night-vision goggles—special eyewear that allows the user to see in the dark

TO LEARN MORE

AT THE LIBRARY

Faust, Daniel R. *Military Drones*. New York, N.Y.: PowerKids Press, 2016.

Gordon, Nick. *U.S. Army*. Minneapolis, Minn.: Bellwether Media, 2012.

Winter, Max. *The Afghanistan War*. Mankato, Minn.: Child's World, 2015.

ON THE WEB

Learning more about peacekeeping is as easy as 1, 2, 3.

1. Go to www.factsurfer.com.

2. Enter "peacekeeping" into the search box.

3. Click the "Surf" button and you will see a list of related web sites.

With factsurfer.com, finding more information is just a click away.

INDEX

Afghanistan, 4

armies, 16, 18

armored vehicles, 15

binoculars, 12

bombs, 6

conflict, 10

drones, 13

fighting, 10, 15

governments, 8, 17, 19

guard, 17

guns, 15

help, 10, 20

land mines, 4, 6, 7

languages, 18

missions, 15, 21

night-vision goggles, 12

peace, 8, 14, 21

police, 10

real-life peacekeeping
    (Egypt and Israel), 11

safety, 8, 17, 21

skills, 18, 20

soldier profile, 17

training, 10, 16, 18

United Nations, 14

U.S. Army, 4

war, 8, 20